THE VETERANS MEMOIR

TRUE COMBAT STORIES FROM WORLD WAR II

MODERN DAILY

Don't Forget Your Free Bonus Downloads!

As our way of saying thank you, we've included in every purchase bonus gift downloads. If you've enjoyed reading this book, please consider leaving a review.

Or Scan Your Phone to open QR code

THE
VETERANS
MEMOIR

TRUE COMBAT STORIES
FROM WORLD WAR II

MODERN DAILY

The Veterans Memoir
True Combat Stories from World War II

CONTENTS

WWII BATTLE HEROES

INSPIRING YOU WITH STORIES OF COURAGE

World War II (WWII) was one of the most crucial and brutal wars in human history, spanning from 1939 to 1945. During this time, countless heroes emerged from the turmoil of battle, showing tremendous courage, determination, and sacrifice. These battle heroes, both men and women, continue to motivate generations of children and adults with their stories of courage and strength. You as boys and girls from a modern generation can learn important lessons from the victories and sufferings of these extraordinary people. You will be fascinated by the tales of these WWII heroes that will resonate with you, offering valuable lessons in strength, compassion, and the importance of standing up for what is right and true.

You will read about and admire heroes of battle and resistance. John Basilon, Audie Murphy, Violette Szabo, Charles Upham, Desmond Doss, and others.

There were also many people or groups of people who did not fit into the traditional war hero role but remained beacons of inspiration for all people.

One example is Anne Frank, a young Jewish girl, who

symbolizes the strength and hope that prevail even during the darkest times of WWII. You should read her diary, written while hiding from the Nazis in Amsterdam and be inspired by it. Despite the looming danger, Anne Frank kept an optimistic outlook and believed in the goodness of humanity. Although her story had a sad ending, it served to remind you and all young people about the power of hope and the significance of adopting standards of diversity and compassion.

Sir Nicholas Winton is another example of compassion. This British humanitarian saved the lives of 669 Jewish children by overseeing their escape from Nazi-occupied Czechoslovakia. His story of selflessness and compassion will inspire you to be kind, compassionate, and to help others in times of need. Winton's act of heroism reminds us that even a single person can make a substantial difference in the lives of others.

Another group which served without fighting were the fearless war nurses. Amid the turmoil of war, nurses showed vast courage and dedication, risking their lives to attend to injured soldiers on the frontlines. These women and a few men demonstrated strength, compassion, and a strong sense of duty. They inspired young girls to pursue their dreams, even in challenging, male-dominated fields and even nowadays they can inspire you to find a career in the service of others. The heroic actions of these nurses show the impact of nurturing and caregiving, encouraging you to adopt roles of empathy and compassion in your own life.

Finally there were the great leaders of the war. While these men did not physically fight, they were blooded heroes from other wars and were chosen to lead their countries in this. One great example is Winston Churchill, the Prime Minister of Britain during WWII. He demonstrated unyielding courage and strength in leading his nation through the most dreadful days of the war. His famous speeches and strong leadership provided confidence and inspiration to the British people and the world at large. His story can teach you about the power of words, strong leadership, and unwavering strength in the face of hardship.

The stories of WWII battle heroes will captivate and inspire you, instilling important values and shaping you not being compassionate, resilient, and responsible citizens. Whether it's the bravery of Anne Frank, the selflessness of Sir Nicholas Winton, or the indomitable spirit of Sir Winstin Churchill or the courage in Battle in the face of terrible danger, the courage of these heroes will leave a memorable mark on your heart,, motivating you to stand up for justice, embrace diversity, and never lose hope in the face of adversity. As we remember and celebrate the legacy of these remarkable people, we need to make sure that their inspiring stories continue to echo through the generations, inspiring you to become heroes in your own right.

AI-Generated Artwork
Illustrative Purposes Only

The Battle of Guadalcanal was a pivotal moment in Sergeant John Basilone's military career, where his heroic actions would come to the forefront. In October 1942, as part of the 7th Marine Regiment, 1st Marine Division, John found himself in a critical defensive position on the island of Guadalcanal in the Pacific.

Amidst the dense jungle, John and his gun team were assigned to hold a narrow pass against a relentless onslaught from the Japanese forces. The pass was a vital strategic position, and its defense was paramount to the success of the overall mission.

1

THE BATTLE OF GUADALCANAL

JOHN BASILONE - A SOLDIER UNTIL THE VERY END

John Basilone was born on November 4, 1916, in Buffalo, New York, to Salvatore Basilone and Dora Bencivenga. He was raised in a close-knit Italian-American community, surrounded by a big extended family. John was the sixth of ten children, and from a young age, he learned the importance of family, hard work, and persistence.

Growing up in Buffalo, John had a modest and humble childhood. His father was a contractor, while his mother dedicated her time to raising their large family. The Basilone household was filled with love, laughter, and a strong sense of companionship.

John's childhood was marked by his love for sports and his natural athleticism. He excelled in football and was admired for his strength and determination on the field. Despite his talent in sports, John's path took an unexpected turn when the Great Depression hit the country, affecting his family's financial situation.

To support his family, John left school at the age of 15 and began working odd jobs. However, he never lost sight of his dreams and goals. He believed in the power of education and self-improvement, so he continued his studies through night school and voraciously read books whenever he had the opportunity.

In 1934, seeking new opportunities, John moved to Raritan, New Jersey. It was there that he began to discover his true calling – the military. Inspired by stories of heroism and patriotism, John enlisted in the United States Marine Corps in 1939. His determination to join the Marines marked the beginning of an incredible journey that would change the course of his life.

TRAINING FOR THE WAR

John Basilone's military training was rigorous and demanding, preparing him to become a skilled and disciplined Marine. From the moment he enlisted in the United States Marine Corps, he grasped the challenges and opportunities that lay ahead, devoting himself wholeheartedly to his training.

During his preliminary training, John underwent an extensive program designed to shape him into a capable and tough soldier. He learned the basic skills of military life, including physical exercise, marksmanship, tactical strategies, and military discipline. The training emphasized the importance of teamwork, leadership, and allegiance to the core values of the Marine Corps.

Physical fitness was a cornerstone of John's training. He underwent grueling physical workouts that tested his stamina, strength, and mental fortitude. Long runs, obstacle courses, and extensive strength training pushed him to his limits, enabling the physical resilience essential for combat.

As part of his training, John learned to handle several weapons and engage in live-fire exercises. He became skilled in handling rifles, machine guns, and grenades, honing his marksmanship skills through regular practice and simulated combat strategies. The training emphasized accuracy, speed, and the ability to function effectively under high-stress circumstances.

Tactical training played a significant role in preparing John for the challenges he would face on the battlefield. He learned to navigate various terrains, conduct tactical movements, and coordinate with his fellow Marines. The training simulated combat strategies, teaching him how to respond and make decisions shortly and effectively.

In addition to combat skills, John received instruction in military protocols, regulations, and discipline. He learned the importance of following orders, maintaining a sense of duty, and upholding the highest standards of integrity and professionalism. The training instilled in him a deep sense of loyalty to his fellow Marines and the standards of the Marine Corps.

Throughout his training, John's outstanding leadership qualities and natural proficiency stood out. His commanders recognized his potential and assigned him positions of responsibility. He was chosen for specialized training, including non-commissioned officer programs, where he further expanded his leadership skills and broadened his knowledge of tactics and strategies.

However, it was not only the technological and physical aspects of training that shaped John as a Marine. The training instilled in him a sense of companionship, brotherhood, and a deep respect for his fellow Marines. He formed bonds with his comrades, recognizing that their lives would depend on one another in the turmoil of combat.

John Basilone's military training laid the foundation for his future heroism and valor. It readied him mentally, physically, and emotionally for the challenges he would face on the battlefield. The discipline, skills, and values instilled during his training shaped him into a tough Marine, ready to serve his country with unflinching commitment and bravery.

John's training not only prepared him with the essential tools for combat but also fostered a sense of honor, duty, and unselfishness that would define his military service. His training served as a testament to the Marine Corps' commitment to producing elite warriors who illustrate the highest ideals of service and sacrifice.

Ultimately, John's military training prepared him for the

conflicts he would face in the Pacific Theater during World War II. It molded him into the hero and legend that he would become, permanently inscribing his name in the annals of Marine Corps history.

THE BATTLE OF GUADALCANAL

The Battle of Guadalcanal was a pivotal moment in Sergeant John Basilone's military career, where his heroic actions would come to the forefront. In October 1942, as part of the 7th Marine Regiment, 1st Marine Division, John found himself in a critical defensive position on the island of Guadalcanal in the Pacific.

Amidst the dense jungle, John and his gun team were assigned to hold a narrow pass against a relentless onslaught from the Japanese forces. The pass was a vital strategic position, and its defense was paramount to the success of the overall mission.

As dusk settled over the battleground, John's gun team readied themselves for the imminent attack. The tension in the air was palpable as they tightened their grips on their weapons and glanced at one another, their eyes reflecting a mix of determination and apprehension.

John, standing tall and resolute, addressed his men. "Alright, listen up! We've got one job to do, and that's to hold this pass. We can't let those enemy forces break through. Stick to your positions, stay focused, and watch each other's backs. We've trained for this. I have faith in each and every one of you. Let's do this!"

The men nodded, their resolve renewed by John's inspiring words. They spread out, positioning themselves strategically along the narrow passage, their guns at the ready.

As darkness engulfed the battleground, the silence was shattered by the sound of enemy footsteps. The Japanese soldiers, determined to breach the Marine defenses, launched a ferocious assault.

John's gun team sprang into action, their weapons roaring to life. Gunfire erupted, illuminating the night sky and casting an eerie glow over the scene. The air filled with the acrid scent of gunpowder as the sound of bullets pierced through the darkness.

"Keep firing! Don't let up!" John shouted above the din, his voice a commanding presence in the chaos. He skillfully operated his machine gun, unleashing a torrent of bullets toward the advancing enemy, forcing them to seek cover.

The Japanese soldiers, undeterred, continued their relentless assault, their own gunfire filling the air. John's gun team fought back with unwavering determination, their coordinated fire holding the enemy at bay.

As the battle raged on, the intensity escalated. Explosions rocked the pass as grenades were lobbed back and forth. John's leadership remained steady, his voice a beacon of reassurance amidst the chaos.

"Basilone! We're running low on ammo!" one of his men

called out.

John glanced at the dwindling supply of ammunition and made a quick decision. "Alright, keep firing, but conserve your shots. We're not going to let them through."

The men nodded, understanding the gravity of the situation. With each shot, they made every bullet count, carefully picking off enemy combatants while conserving their precious resources.

The night wore on, and the battle continued to rage. Fatigue gnawed at the men, but their spirits remained unyielding. They fought not only for themselves but for their fellow Marines, for their country, and for the belief that they were a part of something greater.

Finally, as the first rays of dawn broke through the darkened sky, the enemy assault began to wane. The Japanese forces, unable to penetrate the Marine defenses, began to retreat.

John's gun team breathed a collective sigh of relief, their faces smeared with dirt and sweat. They had successfully defended the narrow pass against overwhelming odds, their resilience and unwavering courage prevailing.

"Good work, men," John said, his voice filled with pride. "We held our ground, and we held it together. We can be damn proud of what we accomplished here today."

The men nodded, their fatigue momentarily forgotten as they basked in the satisfaction of a hard-fought victory. They had fought bravely, not just for themselves but for the ideals they held dear.

In the aftermath of the Battle of Guadalcanal, Sergeant John Basilone's heroism and leadership during the defense of the narrow pass would earn him the Medal of Honor. His actions stood as a testament to the unwavering dedication and sacrifice of the Marines who fought alongside him, forever etching their names in the annals of military history.

POST-WAR

After his heroic actions during the Battle of Guadalcanal, John Basilone returned to the United States as a celebrated hero. His courage and leadership had made a significant impact on the outcome of the battle and garnered admiration from his fellow Marines and the nation as a whole.

Upon his return, John embarked on a national tour to promote war bonds and boost morale. He was hailed as a symbol of valor and patriotism, speaking at rallies and events across the country. Despite the accolades and attention, John remained humble, always acknowledging the sacrifices of his fellow Marines.

However, the war was far from over, and John's desire to continue serving led him to request reassignment. He was deployed to the Pacific once again, this time to Iwo Jima in February 1945. It was during this battle that tragedy struck.

On February 19, 1945, while leading his troops, John Basilone was killed in action. During fierce combat, he valiantly fought alongside his fellow Marines, refusing to back down. His selflessness and bravery in the face of danger continued to inspire those around him.

John's death was a devastating loss to the Marines and the nation. He was posthumously awarded the Navy Cross for his actions on Iwo Jima, further solidifying his legacy as one of the Marine Corps greatest heroes.

In recognition of his exceptional service and sacrifice, the U.S. Navy honored John by naming a destroyer escort after him – the USS Basilone. The ship served as a tribute to his memory and a reminder of the extraordinary bravery displayed by the men and women who fought in World War II.

John Basilone's legacy continues to inspire future generations. His unwavering dedication, heroism, and selflessness have earned him a place among the most revered and respected figures in American military history. His sacrifice serves as a reminder of the countless brave men and women who have given their lives to protect freedom and uphold the values we hold dear.

Though John's life was tragically cut short, his impact will forever be remembered. His memory lives on in the hearts and minds of those who recognize the immense courage and sacrifice that he and his fellow servicemen displayed during World War II.

AI-Generated Artwork
Illustrative Purposes Only

It was during the Battle of Crete in May 1941 that Upham's tremendous courage and leadership abilities first came to the forefront.

The Battle of Crete was an important military engagement that took place during World War II on the Greek island of Crete. The battle occurred from 30 May to 1 June 1941, and pitted German forces against Allied troops, largely consisting of British, Australian, and New Zealand forces, of which Charles Upham was a proud member.

2

THE BATTLE OF CRETE

CHARLES HAZLITT UPHAM - THE PRIDE OF NEW ZEALAND

BEFORE THE WAR

C harles Hazlitt Upham was a distinguished New Zealand soldier and one of the most decorated military personnel in the history of the British Commonwealth. He was born on 21 August 1908, in Christchurch, New Zealand, He was a man who would go on to serve with courage and distinction during World War II. His courage and extraordinary achievements on the battlefield earned him two Victoria Crosses (VC). A Victoria Cross is the highest and most honorable and prestigious award for gallantry in the face of the enemy. The fact that he received two Victoria Crosses is a spectacular achievement.

Charles Hazlitt Upham grew up in a rural farming community. He was the son of a farming family. He spent his childhood in New Zealand and was educated at Christ's College in Christchurch. He had a keen love for adventure and the great outdoors. His childhood experiences stood him well in later years, as he became an excellent horseman and was skilled with firearms.

Charles' parents were John and Agatha Upham. Charles was one of six children in the Upham family. He had two brothers, Harold and Bernard, and three sisters, Margaret, Isabel, and Mary.

One popular story is that, as a child, Charles Upham showed a strong sense of determination and independence. When he was around eight or nine years old, he and his young brother were playing in a paddock on their family farm.

While they were exploring the paddock, Upham glimpsed a huge, aggressive bull that had wandered from its yard and was now charging toward his little brother, who was unaware of the coming danger. Responding quickly, Upham ran towards his brother, yelling and waving his arms to distract the bull's attention away from the boy.

By being so brave and daring, Upham managed to divert the bull long enough for his brother to escape. However, Charles himself was not as lucky. The bull caught up to him and caused a serious injury, goring him in the thigh. Despite his pain from the injury, the brave young Charles Upham showed extraordinary strength and crawled to safety. Fortunately, being young and strong, he recovered from the incident quickly.

This story from Charles Upham's childhood shows us

his courage, quick thinking, and unselfishness, pointing to the incredible bravery he would show later in life during the many battles in which he was involved.

Upham was not only physically powerful but he was also a skillful athlete. He excelled in sports like cricket, rugby, and boxing during his school days and later when he represented his university in rugby

Before the war, Charles Upham labored as a sheep farmer in New Zealand. His experience of farming life and his physical power and endurance were important assets during his military career.

TRAINING FOR THE WAR

Charles Upham joined the New Zealand armed forces in 1939 and was appointed to the 20th Battalion of the 2nd New Zealand Expeditionary Force. He started his military career as a private and quickly showed outstanding leadership skills and courage. His potential was recognized by his commanding officers and he was selected for officer training and commissioned as a second lieutenant in 1941.

Upham's military training took place in New Zealand and the United Kingdom. He underwent tough instruction in infantry tactics, marksmanship, leadership, and other crucial military skills. Upham became known for his physical toughness and unwavering determination. These character traits would define him throughout his career as a soldier and for the rest of his life.

Upham saw action in Greece and Crete before his unit was sent to North Africa

It was during the Battle of Crete in May 1941 that Upham's tremendous courage and leadership abilities first came to the forefront.

The Battle of Crete was an important military engagement that took place during World War II on the Greek island of Crete. The battle occurred from 30 May to 1 June 1941, and pitted German forces against Allied troops, largely consisting of British, Australian, and New Zealand forces, of which Charles Upham was a proud member.

Charles Upham was standing outside his tent, seizing a moment to have a quiet cigarette. As he gazed at the evening sky he was horrified to see the sky filled with parachutes and gliders, bringing troops noiselessly onto Crete.

"I need to alert the commander straight away, " he said to himself, giving a small whistle of dismay as he realized that a terrible battle was about to begin.

Charles Upham went to report the influx of German troops onto the beautiful island of Crete, little realizing that the battle to follow would make him famous.

The German army fought hard. In a short time they had taken over several airfields but Charles Upham and his men were among other Allied soldiers who were determined to fight back.

"Come on men, " Charles whispered as they crept down an alleyway.

A dark-eyed woman kept watch for them as they made their way towards a small church where the German invaders had made barracks. The Cretan population played a crucial role in the resistance, helping the Allies by providing information and joining resistance groups. Charles Upham and his men managed to enter the church by a back door which one of the Cretan women opened for them.

"Get them, men, don't allow anyone to escape or we'll have the whole of Berlin on to us," Charles shouted,

rushing into the church where the German soldiers were resting on bunks on the floor, and throwing a hand grenade into the crowd of soldiers There was a massive explosion and smoke filled the room. The Germans struggled up but were quickly killed by Charles and his men carrying bayonets and knives.

On 22 May 1941, Charles Upham wrote in his diary, "I find myself in the hospital tent after the skirmish today. We came under heavy attack at the Maleme Airfield. We could hardly see or hear because of the noise and the smoke. My men were falling. I know I got shrapnel in my arm sometime during the battle. I was struggling to move easily but I could not leave the men, not after young Anderson was shot. I know that one or two of the lads helped me drag him to safety. We didn't let them get away with much. And at least young Anderson can write his weekly letter home to his mum."

On 30 May Charles Upham found himself in combat again.

"Come on lads, " he shouted encouragement to his men.

The fighting was fierce when Charles was shot through the elbow.

"I can't let them stop me, " he muttered to himself as he dragged himself on his stomach, nauseous from the pain. Although his arm was pouring blood and he could hardly see through the smoke and his vision was blurred from pain, Charles single-handedly destroyed two machine gun posts. His commander praised the injured man when he was brought in by his comrades.

"Your courage and determination have inspired us all, Upham," he said. Your actions have played a crucial role in slowing down the German advance and buying time for your comrades to be evacuated from the island."

In recognition of his extraordinary bravery and leadership during the Battle of Crete, Charles Upham was awarded a Victoria Cross.

In 1942, Upham was sent to fight in the deserts of North Africa, where he displayed outstanding courage during the Battle of Ruweisat Ridge. Despite being injured again, he led his platoon through severe enemy fire, single-handedly destroying several German machine-gun positions and vehicles. His fierce determination and disregard for his safety were instrumental in the achievements of his unit. For his efforts during this battle, Upham was awarded a Bar to his Victoria Cross, making him one of only three people in history to receive this honor.

Later in 1942, Upham was captured by German forces during the Battle of El Alamein and spent the rest of the war as a prisoner of war (POW). Despite being held in captivity, Upham continually attempted to escape and made life hard for his captors. His defiance and refusal to cooperate earned him the admiration of both his fellow POWs and the German soldiers guarding him.

After a failed escape attempt while recovering in an Italian hospital, he was transported to Germany in September 1943. An extremely bold solo attempt to scale his camp's barbed-wire fences in the middle of the day saw Upham become the only New Zealand combatant officer sent to the infamous Colditz camp for habitual escapers in 1944. Colditz Castle is built high above the surrounding land and is surrounded by thick stone walls. When it was commissioned as a POW prison, it was staffed by many guards and anyone who escaped had to travel 400 miles through unfriendly territory. Charles Upham found himself in good company. Although he never escaped from Colditz, there were 130 attempted escapes of which 32 allied soldiers reached safety.

After the war, Upham returned to New Zealand and settled on a farm near Christchurch. His Victoria Cross and Bar were presented to him in person by King George VI during a visit to England in 1946. Upham's exceptional wartime achievements and the honor bestowed upon him made him a national hero in New Zealand.

In addition to his military honors, Upham was also granted the United States Silver Star, making him the only non-American to earn this prestigious award for courage. His remarkable military career and the sheer courage and strength he showed on the battlefield have made him an iconic figure in New Zealand's military history.

After the war, Charles Upham returned to New Zealand and continued with his civilian life. He initially worked as a farmer, overseeing a property in the Cheviot area of North Canterbury. He was known for his humility and hesitation to discuss his wartime experiences.

In the later years of his life, Upham became involved in public service and held several positions. He served as a member of the National Roads Board and the National Parks Authority. Additionally, he worked as a land development officer for the New Zealand government.

Despite his wartime heroism, Upham remained a humble and private individual. Upham married his wife, Molly McTamney, in 1945, shortly after the war. They had three children together and settled on the farm near

Christchurch, New Zealand, where Upham resumed his farming career. He declined numerous offers for commercial endorsements and seldom spoke about his military accomplishments.

Upham's dedication to his country and his acts of valor during World War II made him an icon of New Zealand's military history.

Charles Upham passed away on November 22, 1994, at the age of 86. His legacy as one of the most decorated soldiers in Commonwealth history, and his unwavering courage and determination in the face of danger, continue to inspire generations of New Zealanders.

AI-Generated Artwork
Illustrative Purposes Only

In 1944, Doss was deployed to the Pacific war arena, specifically to the Battle of Okinawa. It was during this difficult and vicious battle that Doss's extraordinary acts of bravery and kindness came to the forefront. Despite the continual bombardment of enemy fire, Doss bravely ventured into the battlefield to rescue wounded soldiers, carrying them to safety and giving them critical medical attention.

3

THE BATTLE OF HACKSAW RIDGE

DESMOND DOSS - THE HERO WHO CARRIED NO WEAPON

Desmond Doss was an incredible person who became well-known and respected for his commitment to his principles and his amazing heroism during World War II. Born on 7 February 1919, in Lynchburg, Virginia, Desmond Thomas Doss grew up in a very religious Seventh-day Adventist family. His early life experiences and strong religious upbringing played a major role in making him a man with strong character and values. Seventh-day Adventists take the commandments very seriously, particularly the two about keeping the Sabbath (Saturday) holy and not taking human life. This created a problem for Seventh-day Adventists, including Doss, when they were conscripted into the US Army.

Desmond Doss grew up in a humble household. He was the son of a carpenter named William Doss and his wife Bertha.

During his childhood, Doss faced various challenges which made him a very determined person. He was a delicate child and was often bullied, but he never allowed these problems to prevent him from believing in nonviolence and a strong belief that life was sacred. These beliefs shaped his incredible actions.

As a child, Desmond Doss exhibited a deep sense of empathy and compassion toward others. He was very upset if he saw any violence and developed a strong hatred of it. These experiences, coupled with his religious beliefs, made him become a strict pacifist (a person who loves peace and refuses to fight).

In his teenage years, Doss faced challenges due to his beliefs. He was ridiculed and even physically bullied by his friends for refusing to be involved in activities that went against his pacifist principles. However, he remained steady and never wavered in his belief in non-violence.

As a young man, Doss worked in a local lumber yard to support his family. Despite facing the pressures and criticism of society, Doss remained steady in his decision to join World War II as a conscientious objector. Desmond's religious beliefs forbade him to carry a weapon or take another person's life. This choice made his road through military training different and challenging.

In 1942, during the Second World War, Desmond Doss enlisted in the United States Army. However, due to his conscientious objection to carrying weapons, he asked to serve as a medic. He also refused to do any work on Saturday, which was his Sabbath. Despite facing initial suspicion and resistance, Doss's unwavering determination ultimately led to his acceptance into the army as a conscientious objector.

During his training, Doss faced various challenges and discrimination for his refusal to bear arms. He was subjected to harsh criticism and resentment from fellow soldiers and superiors. However, Doss's strength and strict commitment to his beliefs eventually won over his comrades and he gained their respect.

Desmond impressed his comrades with his decision to serve as a medic, wanting to save lives rather than take them.

Desmond Doss's early life laid the foundation for the extraordinary acts of heroism he would display during his time in the military. His upbringing, combined with personal experiences, shaped his personality, determination, and unwavering commitment to his beliefs. These qualities would later make him an inspiring person and earn him distinction as one of the most decorated soldiers in American history.

In 1944, Doss was deployed to the Pacific war arena, specifically to the Battle of Okinawa. It was during this difficult and vicious battle that Doss's extraordinary acts of bravery and kindness came to the forefront. Despite the continual bombardment of enemy fire, Doss bravely ventured into the battlefield to rescue wounded soldiers, carrying them to safety and giving them critical medical attention.

His actions were completely heroic. Doss repeatedly braved enemy fire, refusing to seek cover, powerless to defend himself, as he selflessly cared for his injured comrades. He worked day and night tirelessly, risking his own life to protect as many lives as possible. His commitment to his beliefs and his incredible acts of courage earned him the admiration and affection of his fellow soldiers.

Doss's most significant act of valor came during the Battle of Hacksaw Ridge. Despite the sheer confusion and danger of the battlefield, Doss single-handedly saved 75 wounded soldiers from the cliff, lowering them down the steep ridge face to safety. He used a rope sling which he would tie around the injured soldier and then lower them down a cliff to a safer location. Doss would gently guide the wounded soldier down while retaining a firm grasp on the rope, ensuring their descent was as controlled and comfortable as possible. Does using a special double bowline knot which he discovered accidentally during training.

Doss's physical strength and endurance were crucial in performing these risky maneuvers. He possessed tremendous stamina and determination, allowing him to run across rough terrain while carrying and supporting wounded soldiers. His actions certainly saved many lives and earned him great admiration among his comrades.

Imagine the scene at Okinawa at Hacksaw Ridge, a rock plateau 500 feet above safety. The sheer rock face could only be climbed with ropes or rock climbing equipment. There under heavy fire, Desmond Doss asked a comrade to help him lift a particularly heavy soldier. Usually, he managed on his own.

"Thank you, John. I appreciate your help. It's pretty harrowing listening to the shell fire just above us, " Doss said as he lifted a burly soldier into the sling trying to ignore the pain from his wounds.

"No problem, Doss. Just doing my job. You're lucky to be alive after that last assault, " John panted from the exertion of lowering the man to his comrades below.

"I can't take all the credit. As my Daddy used to tell me, someone up there is watching over me. I've never seen anything like this before though. The carnage is unimaginable."

"Yeah, it's a brutal battlefield out here. But you, Doss, you're something else. You're out there, risking your life without a weapon, saving as many men as you can. It's incredible." John sounded humbled as he looked at his comrade.

"Well, I made a promise to myself and God that I would never touch a weapon or take a life. I want to do my part, but I can't compromise my beliefs, "

"I respect that, Doss. Not everyone can stay true to their principles in the heat of battle. It takes a lot of courage to do what you're doing, " A massive explosion caused dust and rocks to rattle down the cliff.

There was a terrible groaning from a group of injured men lying waiting on the rock face. They had been showered with rocks and debris as a missile exploded close to the rockface.

"We need to renew our efforts, John. The cliff face is unstable. These men deserve a chance to go home. There are so many wounded, so much pain." Doss sounded discouraged for a moment. Then he renewed his efforts to lower the wounded men to safety.

"Come on then, " John said, trying another man into the makeshift harness. "Let's get the last of these soldiers down to the medics below.

"Don't struggle soldier, " Doss reproved a very young man gently, his face streaked with blood, sweat, and tears. "Let's lower you to safety."

He attempted to lower the young man who was clinging frantically to him.

"Don't do that, son, " Doss cautioned, "Or I'll put

someone else in your place."

The young man went limp and stopped struggling and Doss managed to lower him to safety.

During his service, Desmond Doss suffered severe injuries, including being injured by a grenade and being hit by sniper fire. Despite his injuries, he proceeded to treat and evacuate wounded soldiers until he could obtain proper medical attention himself.

For his outstanding bravery and compassion, Desmond Doss was awarded the Medal of Honor, the highest military decoration in the United States. He became the first conscientious objector to earn this prestigious award.

POST-WAR

After the war, Doss returned to his hometown of Lynchburg, Virginia as a decorated war hero. He married Dorothy Schutte, and they had one child together. Doss, however, struggled with the emotional and psychological scars left by the war but he continued to live a life dedicated to helping other people. He also suffered from severe loss of hearing which eventually became complete deafness which was a terrible blow to him. Nonetheless, he continued his work as a carpenter and later became a counselor for veterans suffering from PTSD. While Desmond Doss suffered traumatic events during his service, there is limited data available about his particular experiences with post-traumatic stress disorder (PTSD). After the war, he faced challenges adjusting to civilian life and reportedly struggled with nightmares and emotional distress. This a why he decided to counsel other soldiers. However, in those days, PTSD was not recognized and men suffering from it were likely to be told to "man up" or "count their blessings." Recognizing the symptoms and understanding PTSD were less developed during that time, and the term PTSD was only coined years after the war ended.

Desmond Doss passed away on 23 March 2006, at the age of 87. His extraordinary story continues to motivate countless people around the world. His persistent commitment to his faith, his acts of incredible bravery, and his compassion for his fellow human beings make him a true hero whose legacy will endure for generations to come.

Desmond Doss's life is a testament to the power of unwavering beliefs, the strength of the human spirit, and the effect that one person can have on the lives of others. His story serves as a reminder that true heroism lies not in the weapons we bear but in the kindness and selflessness with which we treat others.

Desmond Doss's incredible story was brought to the big screen in the 2016 film "Hacksaw Ridge," directed by Mel Gibson. Actor Andrew Garfield portrayed Doss, earning critical acclaim and further spreading awareness of his incredible actions.

It's important to note that while Doss's story was portrayed in the 2016 film "Hacksaw Ridge," some cinematic exaggerations were made for storytelling purposes. However, the overall depiction of Doss's heroic actions and his use of a rope system to lower men to safety accurately represent the spirit of his heroic acts during the war.

AI-Generated Artwork
Illustrative Purposes Only

Audie Murphy was assigned to the 15th Infantry Regiment, 3rd Infantry Division, and soon found himself in the middle of battle. His first taste of war was in North Africa, where he illustrated his bravery and quick thinking by single-handedly taking out a German tank with a bazooka.

Audie's outstanding marksmanship and ability to think quickly captured the attention of his superiors. He was soon promoted to the rank of sergeant and was later sent into combat in Italy. During the campaign in Italy, Audie led his men through hazardous terrain and engaged in numerous firefights, displaying extraordinary courage and motivating his fellow soldiers.

4

THE BATTLE OF HOLTZWIHR

AUDIE MURPHY - DYNAMITE COMES IN SMALL PACKAGES

Throughout history, there are few stories as amazing and inspiring as that of Audie Murphy. Despite facing enormous challenges, he rose above hardship to become a true American hero. Audie's incredible courage and unwavering strength in the face of danger earned him the distinction of being the most decorated soldier of World War II. This is the incredible tale of Audie Murphy, a young Texan who became a symbol of courage, resilience, and sacrifice for generations to come.

Audie Leon Murphy was born on 20 June 1925, in Kingston, Texas. His boyhood was marked by scarcity and poverty, as he grew up in a sharecropper's family during the Great Depression. After the death of his father, Emmett Murphy, Audie took on the duty of providing for his mother Josie, and his siblings from a young age. Audie was the seventh of twelve children.

Despite these difficulties, Audie's unbeatable spirit and love for adventure led him to wish to become a soldier. However, because he was small (only 5'5") and underage, he was unable to get into the army until his older sister forged his birth certificate which allowed him to join the army at 17.

TRAINING FOR THE WAR

Audie Murphy achieved remarkable feats during his military career. His exceptional training played an important role in shaping him into one of the most decorated soldiers in United States history.

Like all soldiers, Audie Murphy began his military adventure with basic training. When he enlisted in the United States Army in 1942, he underwent basic combat training, which aimed to give recruits the basic skills required for military service. This training included physical exercise, marching, marksmanship, and basic military tactics.

After completing basic training, Murphy went in to do advanced infantry training. Here, he received more specialized teaching focused on infantry tactics, weapon proficiency, and squad-level operations. This training improved his combat skills, taught him to work as part of a team, and prepared him for the difficulties he would face on the battlefield.

As Murphy showed leadership potential, he was chosen for leadership development programs. These programs cultivated the skills essential for leading small units of soldiers in combat. Murphy received training in areas such as tactical decision-making, communication, troop coordination, and maintaining morale under difficult conditions.

Alongside his general infantry training, Audie Murphy received specialized training to become a competent soldier in specific areas. For example, he underwent training as a rifleman, which included intensive marksmanship practice and mastery of various firearms. Additionally, he received training in scouting and reconnaissance techniques, which sharpened his proficiency in gathering important information behind enemy lines.

As the war escalated, Murphy's training intensified to equip him for the brutal realities of combat. This involved simulated battlefield exercises, live-fire training, and tactical maneuvers designed to replicate real-world scenarios. The purpose of combat training was to cultivate soldiers' combat instincts, teach them how to respond under fire and prepare them with the techniques necessary to survive and achieve in battle.

In addition to his regular training, Audie Murphy also attended specialized courses to enhance his abilities further. For example, he completed a course in demolitions, which enabled him to deal with explosives and conduct sabotage operations. Such specialized training equipped him with a wider range of skills and made him a more versatile soldier.

Audie Murphy's military training was rigorous and extensive, providing him with the basis necessary to excel in combat. However, it was his outstanding courage, determination, and natural skill for Warcraft that allowed him to make the most of his training and become one of the most decorated soldiers in American history.

BATTLE FOUGHT

Audie Murphy was assigned to the 15th Infantry Regiment, 3rd Infantry Division, and soon found himself in the middle of battle. His first taste of war was in North Africa, where he illustrated his bravery and quick thinking by single-handedly taking out a German tank with a bazooka.

Audie's outstanding marksmanship and ability to think quickly captured the attention of his superiors. He was soon promoted to the rank of sergeant and was later sent into combat in Italy. During the campaign in Italy, Audie led his men through hazardous terrain and engaged in numerous firefights, displaying extraordinary courage and motivating his fellow soldiers.

However, Audie's most significant and well-known accomplishments occurred during the Battle of Holtzwihr in France. On 26 January 1945, his platoon was ambushed by a German infantry company with substantial tank support. Despite being outnumbered and in a weak position, Audie took control and held off the enemy for hours all on his own. He ignored his safety and used several weapons to halt the advance, including a machine gun, rifle, and even a burning tank destroyer. His incredible bravery and strategic strategies saved his comrades and, because he held the enemy until reinforcements arrived, the Germans were forced to retreat.

The drama would have played out something like this. In a makeshift command post near the front lines at Holtzwihr, Captain Johnson, Sergeant Miller, Private Thompson, and Lieutenant Adams were huddled together, reviewing maps and discussing the ongoing battle.

Captain Johnson said "Alright, listen up, gentlemen. The situation at Holtzwihr is dire. The Germans have launched a fierce counterattack, and we're holding on by a thread. And that thread is about to snap. We need someone to hold the line until reinforcements arrive."

"Captain, we have limited options. Most of our men are already engaged in combat. We're stretched thin as it is, " Adams objected.

Sergeant Miller glanced at the maps, "Sir, what about Audie? He's proven himself time and again. If anyone can buy us some time, he can."

"You're right, Miller. Audie has shown outstanding courage and resourcefulness. Private Thompson, find Audie, he'll be in the forefront of the attack somewhere, and bring him here at once."

Audie entered the command post, rifle slung over his

shoulder.

"Captain, you called me from the battlefield? That must be important. What do you need me to do?"

"Audie, we're in a tight spot. The Germans are pushing hard, and we need someone to hold the line until reinforcements arrive. I can't think of anyone better suited for the job than you. It's a long shot soldier but lives depend on it. A lot of lives."

"Captain, I'll do my best. You can count on me, " Audie agreed without hesitating.

"Audie, we believe in you. You've proven yourself time and again. Hold that position at all costs. We're counting on you to buy us some time, " Adams encouraged him.

"Lieutenant, I won't let you down. I'll make sure those Germans regret ever stepping foot on our soil."

Sergeant Miller hands Audie a rough sketch of the area.

"Audie, this is where you'll be holding. It's a crucial position, and we don't have much firepower left. You'll be the difference between victory and defeat."

"I see. Give me a couple of grenades and a few extra rounds. I'll make every shot count."

"Take this radio, Audie. It's your only lifeline to us. Keep us updated on the situation."

Audie strapped the radio to his back, "Captain, Sergeant, Lieutenant, wish me luck. I won't let you down."

Captain Johnson said, "Godspeed, Audie. May you come

back to us unharmed."

Time passed, and the sounds of gunfire and explosions grew louder. Every minute felt like an hour. The men in the command post anxiously waited for updates. Finally, a voice crackled over the radio

"This is Audie. The Germans are hitting us hard, but I'm holding the line. They won't break through, not on my watch."

"That's the Audie we know! Hang in there, soldier. Reinforcements are on their way." Captain Johnson sounded relieved.

The battle raged on, but Audie continued to fight with unparalleled bravery and skill. What felt like hours later, as the sun began to set, Audie's voice came through the radio once more.

"Captain, this is Audie. The Germans have retreated. We held the line!"

"Outstanding job, Soldier! You've saved us all. Hold your position until reinforcements arrive. We'll come for you."

"Don't worry, Captain. I'll be here. You can count on me."

The men in the command post shared smiles of relief and pride, knowing that Audie's heroic stand at Holtzwihr would be remembered for generations to come.

Audie Murphy's tremendous acts of valor did not go unnoticed. He earned many awards and decorations, including the Medal of Honor, which is the highest military honor in the United States. In addition to the Medal of Honor, Audie was also awarded the Distinguished Service Cross, two Silver Stars, the Legion of Merit, three Purple Hearts, and many other awards.

Following the war, Audie returned to the United States as a hero. However, he struggled with post-traumatic stress disorder (PTSD) and found comfort in acting. He starred in various films based on his wartime experiences, such as "To Hell and Back," which became a box office hit and helped raise awareness about the horrors of war.

Audie Murphy's legacy extends far beyond his military service. He used his reputation to support veterans' rights and raise awareness about PTSD, a condition not understood at the time. He testified before Congress, persuading them to give better care and support to soldiers returning from war.

Audie Murphy's life is an inspiration to people of all ages. Despite his humble beginnings and the challenges he faced, he proved that bravery and determination can overcome any obstacle. His unwavering courage and selflessness in the face of danger set an example for generations to come.

Audie Murphy's story teaches us the value of resilience, compassion, and sacrifice. His legacy serves as a reminder of the sacrifices made by men and women in uniform to protect the freedoms we hold dear.

Audie once said, "A true hero isn't measured by the size of his strength but by the strength of his heart." His words capture the essence of his character and the qualities that made him a true hero. Audie Murphy's indomitable spirit continues to inspire and uplift, reminding us that even in the darkest of times, there is always room for bravery and hope. It also shows us that we can start being brave in small things and that our courage will grow as we grow and mature. Every day we are confronted by ways in which we can help others and stand up against injustice. We can use the example of Audie Murphy in our lives.

During her time as an SOE agent, Szabo undertook two missions in occupied France. In June 1944, she parachuted into the Limoges area as part of Operation Gain, providing significant information to the Allies. Her second mission, Operation Salesman, involved organizing resistance endeavors in the Rouen region.

5

OPERATION GAIN

VIOLETTA SZOBA - THE BEAUTIFUL, BRAVE SPY

Violette Szabo was born on 26 June 1921, in Paris, France. She lived a remarkable life characterized by bravery, tenacity, and unwavering determination. As a British Special Operations Executive (SOE) agent during World War II, Szabo illustrated heroism through her selfless deeds and unwavering commitment to the cause of the Allies. Despite facing many challenges and private losses, Szabo's persistent spirit and courage inspired those around her. This story digs into the extraordinary life of Violette Szabo, showing her as an exceptional heroine during the war.

Violette Reine Elizabeth Bushell, known as Violette Szabo after she married Etienne Szabo, was raised in a loving and supportive family in London, England. Her parents, Charles and Reine Bushell, sowed a sense of patriotism and courage in the young Violette, from an early

53

age. Tragically, her father died when she was just four years old. This left a lasting impact on young Violette.

Despite her turbulent childhood, Violette grew into a strong-willed and independent young woman. She was a tomboy, loving ice skating, gymnastics, shooting, and cycling. She attended school in South Kensington and later became a shop assistant selling expensive perfume. Her optimistic personality and her striking beauty caught the eye of a young French officer, Etienne Szabo. She married him in 1940. He was 31 and she was only 19. It was a typical wartime romance, spontaneous and passionate. She also became a land girl and worked in a munitions factory.

TRAINING FOR THE WAR

After the outbreak of World War II, Violette's life changed substantially. After her husband's deployment to the battlefront, Violette sought to become part of the war effort and joined the Auxiliary Territorial Service (ATS). Her talents and strength were soon noticed by the British SOE, an undercover organization focused on spying, sabotage, and reconnaissance.

Sadly her husband was killed in battle and she found herself pregnant. Her husband never saw their baby daughter Tania. After Tania's birth, she left her daughter with her family and continued her training.

In 1944, Szabo began her training as an SOE agent. Her tough training consisted of various skills, including parachuting, firearms use, explosives, and Morse code.

Szabo's outstanding abilities, combined with her fluency in French and English made her an excellent candidate for hazardous missions behind enemy lines. Her language skills were an advantage during her intelligence work and helped her blend in with the local population while on her missions in France

As part of her training, Szabo also underwent parachute training to prepare for her missions. She trained extensively to master the essential skills for parachuting into enemy territory.

BATTLE FOUGHT

During her time as an SOE agent, Szabo undertook two missions in occupied France. In June 1944, she parachuted into the Limoges area as part of Operation Gain, providing significant information to the Allies. Her second mission, Operation Salesman, involved organizing resistance endeavors in the Rouen region.

Szabo's codename was "Louise." This was the name she used to identify herself and communicate with her fellow agents and commanders.

Szabo's most courageous mission occurred in July 1944 when she became part of a team tasked with disrupting German communications in the area of Rouen. Despite facing continual danger and the threat of being caught, she displayed extraordinary bravery and forethought.

There was a great deal of interest in the chain of

command for the heroic work of Violetta Szabo, code name Louise

"Agent Liewer, I heard you were part of Agent Louise's latest mission. How did it go?" Commander Dickenson looked anxious.

"Yes, that's correct, Sir. It was quite an exhilarating mission. Louise, our skilled operative, was commissioned to infiltrate a high-security building to obtain sensitive information.

"Impressive. I've heard she's known for her stealth and intelligence. Tell me more about the mission."

"Well, our mission objective was to obtain classified data regarding a dangerous supplier of arms to the enemy. Real treasonous stuff. Louise's first task was to collect intelligence and recon the facility's layout, guards' patrol routes, and security measures.

"Sounds like an important first step. Did she encounter any difficulties during the reconnaissance phase?"

"Yes, there were a few unexpected challenges. The facility had state-of-the-art surveillance systems and motion sensors, making it difficult to bypass undetected. However, Louise's aptitude for hacking into systems allowed her to disable the security cameras temporarily and neutralize the sensors.

"Impressive. She seems to have been well-prepared. How did she manage to infiltrate the facility?" the Commander asked.

"Louise devised a detailed plan to exploit a weak point in the building's security. She pretended to be a maintenance technician to gain access to the restricted areas, using forged certifications and blending in with the staff using her fluent French and charming attitude. Her attention to detail and ability to maintain her cover was crucial.

"That's some next-level covert operation. What happened once she gained access to the restricted areas?"

"Once inside, Violetta employed her skills in close-quarters combat and stealth to silently neutralize the guards. She made sure to incapacitate them without raising any alarm or arousing others. Fortunately, she has had extensive training and experience in hand-to-hand combat.

"I've always admired her combat skills. What about the retrieval of the classified data?" the Commander asked curiously.

"That was the most intense part. The data was stored in a highly secure server room with multiple layers of encryption. Violetta had to hack into the system while keeping a close eye on the time, as the guards' patrol routes were altered every so often. She managed to overcome the encryption and retrieve the vital information just in time.

"Incredible. She's truly a master of her craft. Was she able to escape without any complications? I have a feeling sometimes that she's living on borrowed time. She's so daring."

"There were a few close calls during the extraction

phase. Louise had to navigate back through the facility while avoiding extra security measures that had been initiated due to the breach. She utilized diversionary tactics and her outstanding agility to evade detection and successfully escaped with the retrieved data." Liewer explained. It was hard to describe how impressive Violetta was when she was on a mission. All her light-hearted, friendliness formed into something fierce and focused. She could not be distracted.

"That sounds like an intense mission. Louise never ceases to astonish me with her capabilities. I'm glad the mission was a success. What's the next step?"

"Now that we have the information, it will be analyzed by our intelligence team. It's anticipated to give critical insights into the arms dealer's systems and network. With this knowledge, we can better target their illegal activities and dismantle their organization before they supply more arms to the Germans.

"Well done, Agent Liewer, Please convey my congratulations to Louise for a job well done."

Unfortunately, however, during this mission, Violetta Szabo's luck ran out, and she was captured by the German forces. She was berries by an ankle that she had injured years before when she and a colleague Dufour attempted to flee German pursuit. Unable to walk, she allowed Dufour to escape by covering the area with gunfire so the Germans could not get close to him. They captured her when her ammunition ran out.

Violette Szabo's unwavering courage did not falter even in custody. She underwent brutal questioning and torture but remained resolute, refusing to reveal any vital evidence that could jeopardize the safety of her comrades and the resistance networks she had helped establish.

Despite being cruelly tortured with beatings, waterboarding (a cruel torture where water is poured over a cloth covering the victim's face, giving the impression of drowning. It causes terrible fear, pain, and panic), and electrical shocks, and being psychologically tormented by sleep deprivation and isolation, Violeta remained strong.

Tragically, after withstanding months of imprisonment and misery, Violette was transferred to Ravensbrück concentration camp. She worked in the Königsberg punishment camp where she and other women felled trees and cleared land for an airfield by hand. They were forced to stand up to 5 hours at a time in roll call dressed in the summer clothes in which they had arrived although winter had arrived. Many of them starved to death. On 5 February 1945, at the age of 23, she was executed by the Nazis. She was shot in the head while kneeling on the ground. She left behind her young daughter, Tania.

Her strength and sacrifice have been widely recognized and honored after she died for her contributions to the war effort.

She was posthumously awarded the George Cross, the

highest award for courage bestowed upon civilians in the United Kingdom. Her name is also immortalized on the Brookwood Memorial in Surrey, England, alongside other courageous SOE agents.

Her daughter Tania, aged just four, received the George Cross from King George VI on behalf of her mother Violette Szoba.

Beyond the awards, Violette's legacy lives on as an encouragement and inspiration to generations to come. Her story has been depicted in various forms of media, including the book "Carve Her Name with Pride" by R.J. Minney and the 1958 film adaptation of the same name.

In 2008, the Royal Mail in the United Kingdom issued a postage stamp featuring Violette Szabo as part of a set honoring Special Operations Executive agents.

Additionally, a blue plaque commemorating her life and heroism was unveiled at her former family home in London. In 2009, a bronze statue of Violette Szabo was unveiled in her hometown of Wormelow Tump, Herefordshire, England. The Violette Szabo Museum, located in Herefordshire, England, also serves as a testament to her incredible life and contributions during World War II.

Violette Szabo's life was tragically cut short, but her unwavering courage and heroism have left a memorable mark on history. Her contributions as an SOE agent and her relentless dedication to the Allied cause continue to inspire people today.

Szabo's resilience in the face of hardship and her responsibility to her comrades illustrates the very essence of heroism. Her selflessness, courage, and unwavering determination make her an iconic figure in the annals of World War II history.

As we reflect on Violette Szabo's courageous life, let us recall the sacrifices she made and the indestructible spirit she symbolized. Her legacy serves to remind us of the incredible bravery shown by many people during times of great darkness, and it motivates us to strive for courage and strength in the face of hardship.

AI-Generated Artwork
Illustrative Purposes Only

The annals of aviation history are filled with stories of extraordinary pilots, but few are as esteemed and celebrated as Saburo Sakai, a World War II fighter ace of the Imperial Japanese Navy. His ability in the skies, his relentless spirit, and his unwavering devotion to the Empire have earned him a well-deserved place as an aviation legend. This article describes the life, battles, and later years of the extraordinary Saburo Sakai, a man whose legacy continues to motivate and fascinate aviation fans worldwide.

6

THE BATTLE OF MIDWAY

SABURO SAKAI: THE LEGENDARY JAPANESE ACE

The annals of aviation history are filled with stories of extraordinary pilots, but few are as esteemed and celebrated as Saburo Sakai, a World War II fighter ace of the Imperial Japanese Navy. His ability in the skies, his relentless spirit, and his unwavering devotion to the Empire have earned him a well-deserved place as an aviation legend. This article describes the life, battles, and later years of the extraordinary Saburo Sakai, a man whose legacy continues to motivate and fascinate aviation fans worldwide.

He was born on 25 November 1916, in Saga Prefecture, Japan. Saburo Sakai's destiny as an ace pilot was set in motion from an early age. His family had a strong affiliation with the Samurai. His ancestors had been Samurai and had been part of the Japanese invasions in Korea in the late 1500s. The family had fallen on hard times and eventually became farmers. Saburo Sakai was the third son of four boys and three sisters. His father died when he was eleven and his mother was left to raise 7 children.

As a young boy, Sakai was captivated by airplanes and dreamed of becoming a pilot. At the age of nine, he had his first flight experience when he was taken on a joyride in a military seaplane by a friend of the family who was a naval officer. This experience left a lasting impression on young Sakai and cemented his desire to fly.

He was sent to school and financed by his mom's brother. He sent him to a Tokyo high school. Unfortunately, he was a poor student and was sent back home to Saga after two years. On 31 May 1933, he enlisted in the Imperial Japanese Navy as a sailor. The discipline was tough and he was often beaten until he passed out but he proved to be a good sailor and was later trained at the naval aviation school in Kagoshima. Sakai's flying skills were apparent from the start, and he rapidly developed a reputation for his outstanding marksmanship and calmness under pressure.

During his flight training, Sakai survived a severe accident that could have ended his aviation career. While practicing aerial techniques, his plane's engine malfunctioned, and he crash-landed. The accident left him with serious injuries and limited vision in one eye, making him ineligible for frontline service. However, his outstanding flying skills and determination persuaded his superiors to allow him to continue as a pilot. Japanese flight training was extremely harsh. There were wrestling matches where winning was everything regardless of injury, acrobatics without a safety net, and prolonged and agonizing swimming training. The success rate was low, with only about a third of trainees qualifying. Sakai was tough and determined, however, and he received a silver watch from the emperor for being the best trainee of his year.

TRAINING FOR THE WAR

As friction escalated in the Pacific during the late 1930s, Sakai's prowess as a fighter pilot was put to the test in the Second Sino-Japanese War. By the time World War II exploded, he was already Petty Officer First Class and was appointed to the aircraft carrier Zuikaku as part of the terrifying Tainan Air Group.

THE BATTLES OF PEARL HARBOR AND MIDWAY

Saburo Sakai's combat debut occurred during the attack on Pearl Harbor on 7 December 1941. Though the Japanese forces accomplished a devastating surprise attack, Sakai's private account of the battle, recorded later, described how he felt sorrow and acknowledged the enormous loss of life and devastation caused during the raid which brought America into the War.

It was during the Battle of Midway, however, that Sakai's skills and resilience truly showed. When engaging in dogfights against American pilots, he showed tremendous staying power and shrewdness. In one amazing encounter, his Zero fighter was badly damaged, and he was blinded in one eye by enemy fire. Despite his injuries, Sakai managed to fly back to his carrier, saving his life and protecting his legacy as a fighter ace

Saburo Sakai's Heroic Stand at Midway

Imagine what it must have been like to be a fighter pilot in a fragile little plane.

This is what a conversation between Saburo Sakai in his Mitsubishi A6M Zero and Ground Control, Masaru, the Radio operator on the Japanese aircraft carrier Akagi.

To set the scene: Saburo Sakai was engaged in a dogfight against American fighter planes during the Battle of Midway. He skillfully maneuvered his Zero through the skies, taking down several enemy planes. Meanwhile, the Ground Control, Masaru provided him with information and support from the Akagi.

"Sakai, this is Masaru. You have multiple contacts at your 12 o'clock. Be careful; it looks like a formation of American fighters." Masaru sounded anxious.

"Masaru, this is Sakai. I see them. I'm diving to engage." Sakai sounded calm and in control.

The dogfight intensified, and Saburo skillfully took down two enemy planes.

"Nice shot, Sakai! You got two of them!"

"Thank you, Masaru. I'm breaking off and climbing back

up."

"Roger that, Sakai. Be aware, there's a Wildcat closing in on your six."

"I see him. I know him. He's a good fighter, but I won't let him take me down."

With accurate maneuvers, Saburo evaded the Wildcat's attacks and fought back, shooting it down.

"Incredible flying, Sakai! You've taken down another one," commented Masaru

"Thanks, Masaru, But don't count them out just yet."

"Understood. We have more American fighters inbound. Be careful."

"I'll be ready. Send me their positions."

Ground Control provided Saburo with updated enemy positions, and he skillfully engaged the incoming fighters, one by one, outmaneuvering them and claiming more victories.

"Sakai, you're doing amazing things up there. Keep it up!"

"I won't disappoint, Masaru. I'll give it my all for the Emperor!"

As the dogfight raged on, Saburo continued to show incredible skill and determination. However, his Zero took some damage during the intense battle.

"Sakai, your plane's taken a hit! Are you alright?"

"I'm fine. My plane can still fly, but I need to disengage for a moment."

"Take your time. We'll cover you."

Saburo carefully withdrew from the main fight and used his expert piloting to minimize the impact of the damage.

"Masaru, I'm ready to rejoin the battle."

"Good to have you back, Sakai. Stay sharp!"

The dogfight continued and Saburo pushed himself to the limits. He managed to take down a few more American planes but realized his ammunition was running low.

"Masaru, I'm almost out of ammo."

"Roger that, Sakai. Head back to the carrier. We'll cover you."

"I'll make my way back. Thank you for the support, "

As Saburo headed back to the carrier, the battle raged on around him. He managed to return safely, having played a crucial role in the fierce aerial combat during the Battle of Midway.

"Sakai, you've done a remarkable job up there. Your bravery and skill will be remembered and honored"

"Thank you, Masaru. It was an honor to serve."

With a sense of pride and accomplishment, Saburo Sakai landed his damaged Zero on the carrier deck, thinking about the intense battle he just fought.

Throughout the war, Sakai continued to collect a

remarkable tally of victories, earning the proud title of "Sakai's 64." He fought in some of the key battles of the Pacific, including Guadalcanal and the Solomon Islands campaign.

Throughout his military career, Saburo Sakai adopted the Samurai code of Bushido. He was known for his politeness and respect for his enemies. On one occasion, after downing an American aircraft, he landed near the crash site to check on the enemy pilot's condition. When he discovered the pilot had died, he paid his respects to the fallen pilot.

Despite his amazing combat record, fate dealt a cruel hand to him during the Battle of Guadalcanal. In August 1942, he was critically wounded after a dogfight with American Wildcats. Against all odds, he managed to crash-land his shattered Zero on the island. Badly injured and abandoned behind enemy lines, Sakai was rescued by a kindly native Solomon Islander who tended to his wounds and saved his life.

Soon after that, Sakai was captured by American forces and faced the challenges of imprisonment, and spent the remaining years of the war in captivity. Despite this obstacle, his unbeatable spirit and polite, courteous behavior earned the respect of his captors and fellow prisoners alike.

After Japan's surrender in 1945, Saburo Sakai returned to a country ravaged by war. His life as a soldier came to an end, but his passion for flying continued. He went on to work as a civilian test pilot, contributing to the post-war aviation industry

Sakai's later years were marked by a genuine commitment to promoting peace and understanding between former enemies. He became a Buddhist and swore never to kill any living thing again. He remarried when his wife died but struggled to find work. He eventually opened a printing shop. He traveled to the United States, creating bonds with American veterans and visiting aviation events where he shared his experiences and understanding of the war. He also became very critical of the war and war generally. He told reporters, soon before his death, that he still prayed for the souls of the enemy pilots had killed.

Sakai wrote an autobiography entitled "Samurai". This gave an interesting insight into the mind of an Aviation warrior. He also won many awards and medals, including the very prestigious Order of The Rising Sun.

On the lighter side, he also helped Microsoft design the very popular game "Combat Flight Simulator 2".

On 22 September, 2000, the world lost a true aviation hero when Saburo Sakai died at the age of 83. His legacy lives on, not only in the many aerial victories he accomplished but also in the spirit of compassion and reconciliation he symbolized.

Saburo Sakai's life journey from a determined young pilot to a celebrated ace and then to a symbol of reconciliation, lives as proof of the endurance of the human spirit. It also shows how human beings mature and develop. Although he had been such a great and ruthless warrior, he became a man who hated war and the loss of life. Through the trials of war he showed unwavering courage and honor, leaving a memorable mark on the history of aviation. The world will always remember this outstanding Japanese fighter ace, Saburo Sakai, whose name remains high among the bright stars of courage and heroism.

Erich Hartmann is a legendary figure in the history of aviation. He was born on 19 April 1922, in Weissach, Württemberg, Germany. He was to become the most successful fighter ace in the history of aerial warfare, claiming an extraordinary 352 aerial victories during World War II. He was nicknamed the "Black Devil" by Soviet forces and his life and battles are a testament to his outstanding skill, determination, and unwavering loyalty to his country

7

THE EASTERN FRONT

ERICH HARTMANN AN AVIATION LEGEND

E rich Hartmann is a legendary figure in the history of aviation. He was born on 19 April 1922, in Weissach, Württemberg, Germany. He was to become the most successful fighter ace in the history of aerial warfare, claiming an extraordinary 352 aerial victories during World War II. He was nicknamed the "Black Devil" by Soviet forces and his life and battles are a testament to his outstanding skill, determination, and unwavering loyalty to his country.

Early Life and Military Career:

Erich Hartmann, also known as "The Blond Knight of Germany," was an outstanding fighter pilot during World War II and is without question the highest-scoring ace in the history of aerial warfare. He was born on 19 April 1922, in Weissach, Germany, he had a relatively ordinary childhood until the rise of Nazi Germany.

During his early years, Erich Hartmann grew up in a supportive family environment. His parents encouraged his interests. He was raised in a small town in Saxony, where his father was a doctor. His fascination with aviation was stimulated at a young age when his family took him to an air show, and he saw the planes in action. The young Erich gazed at the maneuvres of these seemingly fragile aircraft in amazement.

In the 1930s, Adolf Hitler came to power and the Nazi regime began to militarize Germany. The mood in the country changed dramatically. Like many young Germans at the time, Erich Hartmann became influenced by the nationalistic sentiments and the glorification of military service that were part of this era in German history. Erich was part of the Nazi youth movements, as were most other young people at that time.

In 1939, at the age of 17, Hartmann joined the military service. He started as a flight cadet in the Luftwaffe, the German Air Force. He showed extraordinary flying skills during his training, and in 1942, he was appointed to Jagdgeschwader 52, a fighter wing known for its elite pilots. This was one of the most successful German fighter units of the war. He received intensive combat training under experienced pilots, which formed the basis for his future successes

Hartmann's boyhood experiences and upbringing undoubtedly played a role in molding his character and determination, but it was his unique flying talent and relentless quest for excellence that drove him to become the most successful fighter pilot in history with an unbelievable 352 confirmed aerial victories.

HIS ROLE IN THE WAR

Hartmann's baptism of fire came on the Eastern Front, where the Luftwaffe was engaged in fierce aerial combat against the Soviet Air Force. He achieved his first aerial victory on August 5, 1942, when he shot down a Soviet Ilyushin Il-2 ground-attack aircraft. As his experience and skill grew, so did his kill count. By the end of 1942, he had claimed 48 victories, earning him the Knight's Cross of the Iron Cross.

In 1943, Hartmann's accomplishments escalated rapidly. On 29 October, he reached the century mark in aerial victories, becoming the first pilot in history to do so. His success led to his promotion to a Staffelkapitän (squadron leader) in JG 52. Despite the harsh conditions and never-ending combat, he showed modest and disciplined behavior, earning the admiration of his fellow pilots.

Hartmann was not only an extraordinary pilot but also a man of decisive principles. He followed a strict code of conduct, which he pursued throughout his career. Unlike some other aces, he would not claim "easy" victories such as unconfirmed sightings or damaged aircraft. He believed in verifying his kills fully to ensure the accuracy of his record.

This practice earned him the respect of his comrades and later of historians.

Possibly if Erich Hartmann wrote a letter home, and we can assume he did, this is what it might have sounded like. He would not have given away any battle plans or situations because of security but he would have wanted to share his feelings with his mom and dad.

Dear Mutter,

I hope this letter finds you both in good spirits and keeping healthy. I know Papa will be working too hard with his patients, and you, my dear Mutter, are hopefully not being too deprived of food and resources. I wish I could share it with you. We are given excellent provisions but I think they know a hearty meal is necessary to keep us up in the sky all day. I apologize for not writing sooner, but the situation here on the frontlines is very intense. When I finally am debriefed for the day and fall into my bunk, I simply am dead to the world until the next morning. I want to take some time to share with you what has been going through my mind during these difficult times, as I can hardly imagine how worried you must be about me, even though I am all grown up!

As you can imagine, being here in the center of combat is a completely different world. The seriousness of the situation and the duty I owe to my country weighs heavily on my mind. Erich Hartmann is now a name that has become known to many, and I'm constantly reminded of the importance of my actions and decisions on the battlefield. There's an overpowering sense of duty to protect not only my fellow comrades but also our nation and its values. It's hard to believe that just a little while ago, I was just your little boy Bubi, playing with my soccer ball.

In the thick of battle, emotions change rapidly. Fear, for instance, is always present. The understanding that danger is around every corner is ever-present, and that fear reminds me to be careful and vigilant. However, it is important to control fear and turn it into an advantage, as acting out of fear alone could lead to fatal consequences. The lessons in duty that you and Papa taught me and my training help me to keep calm and think rationally even in the most risky situations.

Adrenaline pumps through my veins during battle, waking up my senses and reflexes. The adrenaline rush can be both a gift and a curse; it helps me respond quickly to threats, but it can also cloud my judgment. I think I am a superhero! That's where discipline and experience come into play. Training has drilled into me the importance of following procedures, making planned decisions, and never losing sight of the bigger picture, which will be the victory of our beloved people. I see your dear faces Mutter and Papa and you represent the German people to me. Good people trapped in a war.

Amidst the chaos of war, it's important to remember that people die. I often find myself thinking about the lives affected by our actions - both our enemies and our comrades. It's never easy to take a life, although it seems easier in a plane than when you are fighting in hand-to-hand combat on the ground. It's a bit of a bubble. I have taken many lives. It's something I have thought about a lot. Because I know that my actions will have serious consequences on others my conscience often feels heavy. But then again, I remind myself that it is the nature of war - an unfortunate reality I must face.

Amid the battle, a strange friendship forms among comrades. We rely on each other for backing, and that bond creates an incredible sense of belonging. It's almost as if we form a brotherhood, sharing both the joys of survival and the pain of loss. Losing a comrade can be very heart-wrenching, and one must force oneself to keep pressing forward in their memory.

Despite the craziness and bitterness of the battlefield, I find courage in the belief that what I do here contributes to a greater cause. Protecting our homeland and its people is an honorable and decent pursuit. This thought makes me strong in the toughest of times.

I want you to know that I am doing my best to stay safe and make you proud. I will always stay true to the values and beliefs you have instilled in me throughout my life. Please take care of yourselves. Give my best love to Papa and tell him that the love and support of both of you are what keep me going. May the Gut Gott bless and keep you both.

With love and respect,

Your son "Bubi."

In February 1944, Hartmann was given the Knight's Cross with Oak Leaves, Swords, and Diamonds after the achievement of 200 victories. This recognition showed not only his success in combat but also his leadership skills and understanding of tactics. Despite many offers to be transferred to less dangerous postings or serve as an instructor, he chose to stay on the front lines, flying combat missions with barely a break.

POST-WAR

In May 1945, as Germany faced looming defeat, Hartmann tried to escape to the West with his unit. However, he was forced to surrender to American forces in Austria. The Americans handed him over to the Soviets, who considered him a war criminal because of the cast numbers of Soviet lives he had taken. He suffered years of harsh imprisonment in the Soviet Union, where he was subjected to brutal ill-treatment and forced labor.

After years of captivity, Hartmann was finally released in 1955, following fierce negotiations between the West German government and the Soviet Union. He returned home a hero to many, but some debate surrounded his release, with his critics claiming he had cooperated with the Soviets. However, these reports were never verified, and Hartmann strongly denied any affiliation with his Soviet enemy.

Upon his return to West Germany, Hartmann joined the recently formed West German Air Force (Bundeswehr) and helped with the establishment of its first fighter wing. He continued to serve in the army, reaching the rank of Colonel and flying highly advanced jet aircraft.

Throughout his life, Hartmann stayed active in aviation and the defense community. He served as a consultant for military matters and contributed to the improvement of modern fighter tactics. His legacy as a pilot and an instructor endured, inspiring many generations of aviators.

Erich Hartmann passed away on 20 September 1993, at the age of 71. He left behind a heritage that stays unparalleled in the stories of aviation history. His 352 confirmed aerial victories are proof of his extraordinary skill, bravery, and dedication to his country. Hartmann's faithfulness to his personal code of conduct set him apart from many of his fellow pilots and established his reputation as one of the most respected fighter pilots of all time.

Simo Häyhä, also known as "The White Death," was a celebrated Finnish marksman and a national hero. Born on 17 December 1905, in Rautjärvi, a small municipality in Finland, Häyhä's life was defined by incredible courage, determination, and extraordinary sniper skills. He became well-known for his skill during the Winter War of 1939-1940, where he served as a sniper in the Finnish Army. He achieved phenomenal success against the invading Soviet forces. This story investigates the remarkable life journey of Simo Häyhä, from his modest beginnings to his long standing legacy as the most effective marksman ever.

FINLAND DURING THE RUSSIAN INVASION

SIMO HÄYHÄ: THE WHITE DEATH

The Winter War was a small and rather obscure part of World War II. As part of its expansionist policy, the Soviet Union, before it became an Allied power had signed a treaty with Germany which Hitler did not honor hence the Soviet Union throwing in their lot with Britain and France. In the short period in 1939 when Russia remained uninvolved in War, it was decided to send the might of the Russian army to invade Finland which had a tiny army. The result was that Russia lost nearly 600 000 soldiers, more than the number of the whole Finnish army. It was men of the caliber of Simo Häyhä that made that happen.

Simo Häyhä, also known as "The White Death," was a celebrated Finnish marksman and a national hero. Born on 17 December 1905, in Rautjärvi, a small municipality in Finland, Häyhä's life was defined by incredible courage, determination, and extraordinary sniper skills. He became well-known for his skill during the Winter War of 1939-1940, where he served as a sniper in the Finnish Army. He achieved phenomenal success against the invading Soviet forces. This story investigates the remarkable life journey of Simo Häyhä, from his modest beginnings to his long standing legacy as the most effective marksman ever.

In case you are not sure, a sniper is a highly trained marksman or shooter who specializes in precision shooting over long distances. Snipers use rifles with telescopic sights to engage targets with precision and stealth, often in military or law enforcement operations. Their major goal is to eliminate specific targets with single shots, relying on hiding away and camouflage to remain hidden and avoid detection.

A sniper typically has to reload their rifle after each shot. Snipers use bolt-action rifles, which need to be manually operated to load a new round into the chamber after firing. This process helps them to be accurate and precise.

THE EARLY YEARS

Simo Häyhä was raised in a rural farming district, which instilled in him the values of discipline and hard work from a young age. Growing up, he developed a deep love for hunting and spent countless hours in the outdoors mastering the art of marksmanship. He became especially skilled with the Mosin-Nagant rifle, a weapon that would later become his killing device of choice during the Winter War.

MILITARY SERVICE

When the Soviet Union invaded Finland on 30 November 1939, Häyhä was 33 years old. He immediately enlisted in the Finnish Army to protect his homeland from the hostile invasion. Given his fame as a sharpshooter, he was assigned to the 6th Company of JR 34 (Infantry Regiment 34) and began his journey as a warrior.

The Winter War was characterized by harsh conditions and endless battles, especially in the heavily forested regions of Finland. Häyhä's understanding of the terrain and his extraordinary camouflage skills made him a lethal threat to the Soviet forces. He often hid himself in snow or forest-covered pits, earning his famous nickname, "The White Death," for blending completely with the wintry surroundings.

Simo Häyhä's sniping tactics were both creative and effective. He resisted using a scope on his rifle to keep a low profile and reduce glare that could give away his position. Instead, he relied on the iron sights, becoming incredibly skilled at calculating distances and analyzing weather conditions like wind and temperature. Häyhä also used a technique known as "motti tactics," where he targeted Soviet soldiers in small groups or "mottis," causing psychological stress and panic among the Soviet ranks, as bullets took out small group after small group.

His influence on the Winter War was enormous. Over about 100 days of active combat, Häyhä is believed to have killed over 500 Soviet soldiers. This astounding feat earned him deep respect from his comrades and fear from his enemies. His success in withstanding and staving off the Soviet advance played a hugely important role in boosting Finnish morale during the challenging war.

Imagine the scene on the day that Häyhä apparently killed 25 Soviet soldiers during the six hours of available daylight in the Finnish Winter.

The setting was the snow-covered forests of Finland on a bitterly cold day, 21 December 1939 - the shortest day of the year. Simo Häyhä, the legendary Finnish sniper, was perched on a hidden log, deeply, camouflaged amidst the trees, with his rifle at the ready. The rifle was like an extension of his arm. Without it, he felt lost. The Winter War was in full swing, and the Finnish forces were fiercely protecting their homeland against the invading Soviet Union. They were angry that they had been forced into a conflict, not of their making.

Simo Häyhä whispered these words softly in his head. There was a steely determination in his eyes.

"Today is another day of survival, of protecting this land that we love. The enemy may have misjudged us, but they will soon understand the unbeatable spirit of the Finnish people. The biting cold is a companion to us. This is our home, our terrain, and we know it better than anyone."

He paused for a moment, surveying the surroundings, his eyes keenly scouring for any signs of movement.

"The invaders march on, their hearts are filled with arrogance. They think they have the power. But they do not understand the strength of a nation unified in the face of catastrophe. We are outnumbered and outgunned, but our courage burns like the fire of a thousand suns. Each one of us stands as David against Goliath. We will make our stand and we will make them pay dearly for each Finnish life."

He clenched his fists, his fingers brushing against the trigger of his rifle. He could a distant rustling and he wrinkled his nose in disdain. These idiots blundered through the forest as if they owned it.

"I await my moment. Patience, accuracy, and the will to protect my homeland is all I need. I am but a shadow, a ghost in l the snow. They call me the "White Death." That name was given by this saw a comrade fall beside them touched by my unseen bullet. For every Finnish life lost, I will take as many lives of the enemy as God allows."

He took a deep breath, the frosty air stinging his lungs. They were close now, blundering through the underbrush like wild boar.

"Every shot fired echoes the cries of our ancestors, who fought for this land before us. They may have superior firepower, but we have the knowledge of our home and the cunning of hunters. The snow is our ally, and the forest is our fortress. I am but one of many, and our combined will is unbreakable.

He remembered the faces of his fellow soldiers, his friends and family, and the weight of responsibility weighed heavily on his shoulders. He knew how few Finns there were compared to the might of the Russian army.

"As the Winter War rages on, let it be known that we will not give in. We will not bow down to their dictatorship. Today, on this icy December day, I stand strong, determined to defend my people, my country. My aim is true, and my heart loves Finland."

With his finger resting lightly on the trigger, Simo Häyhä prepared himself for the battle to come. He knew that his actions, and those of his comrades, would shape the destiny of Finland and become a symbol of resistance for generations to come. He raised his rifle and fired again and again, loading so quickly that his movements seemed magical. Man after man fell bleeding into the snow. The Russian soldiers stared wildly into the snowy landscape but they could see no one. Truly the shootist must be a ghost

Häyhä's incredible success as a sniper, however, came at a high price On 6 March 1940, during a military attack he was hit in the jaw by an explosive bullet fired by a Soviet sniper. The trauma was severe, and he was taken to a field hospital, where he slipped in and out of a coma for several days. Despite the grim prognosis, Häyhä recovered and regained consciousness.

The injury, however, left his facial muscles seriously damaged, causing partial facial paralysis. Although he survived, he was unfit to return to the frontline.

Nevertheless, his remarkable contribution to the war effort and his incredible feats in combat garnered him numerous honors and awards, including the Cross of Kollaa, a prestigious Finnish military medal.

POST-WAR LIFE AND LEGACY

Following the Winter War, Simo Häyhä returned to the country, where he led a private life away from the limelight. He settled in Ruokolahti, his hometown, and worked on his farm. He bred dogs and hunted moose. Some people were critical of him but mostly people respected that he had done his best for his country. Despite his amazing fame, Häyhä remained simple and humble, never striving for personal gain or attention for his war efforts.

As time went on, Häyhä's celebrated status grew and became legendary. He became an iconic symbol of Finnish resilience and courage during the Winter War. His name became a symbol of Finnish resistance and the uncompromising spirit of a nation defending its independence.

In his later years, Häyhä liked spending time with his family, friends, and fellow war veterans. He joined in with various events and gatherings to share his experiences and insight with younger generations. His life story inspired stories, documentaries, and even a few films, establishing his place as a national hero and a historical icon for all time.

On 1 April 2002, Simo Häyhä died at the age of 96. The

news of his death reverberated across Finland and even reached global audiences. He was given a state funeral with full military honors, attended by VIPs, military personnel, and countless regular citizens who wished to pay their respects.

The legacy of Simo Häyhä endures to this day. His incredible achievements as a soldier and sniper continue to be commemorated in Finland, and his story serves as a lasting reminder of the resilience of the human spirit in the face of hardship. Häyhä's life and deeds continue to encourage people worldwide, teaching us the value of determination, courage, and being a patriot.

Simo Häyhä, "The White Death," rose from a modest upbringing to become one of the most legendary snipers in military history. His unparalleled skill and bravery during the Winter War assured his place as a national hero in Finland. Häyhä's legacy serves as a testament to the power of individual courage and determination, and his story remains a cherished part of Finland's history. As we remember the life of Simo Häyhä, we honor not only his exceptional marksmanship but also his enduring spirit, which continues to inspire generations to come.

Adrian Carton de Wiart was an outstanding military officer with an extraordinary and adventurous life. Born on 5 May 1880, in Brussels, Belgium, he was the son of an Irish father and a Belgian mother. He was raised in a well-off family and he receive

9

THE BATTLE OF MONTE CASINO

ADRIAN CARTON DE WIART - A DISTINGUISHED WARRIOR

EARLY LIFE

Adrian Carton de Wiart was an outstanding military officer with an extraordinary and adventurous life. Born on 5 May 1880, in Brussels, Belgium, he was the son of an Irish father and a Belgian mother. He was raised in a well-off family and he received a privileged upbringing and an education at some of Europe's finest schools. He also attended Oxford University.

At the age of 16, Adrian Carton de Wiart enlisted in the British Army, joining the Royal Military Academy at Sandhurst. He was commissioned into the British Army's Welsh Regiment in 1899 and began his military career during the Second Boer War in South Africa. It was during this conflict that he was exposed to the terrible realities of war and it marked the beginning of a long and distinguished military journey.

Over the years that followed, Carton de Wiart served in numerous colonial campaigns and conflicts, including in India and Sudan. His bravery and leadership skills were recognized by his superiors and his comrades, earning him promotions and commendations. By the time World War I broke out, he had risen to the rank of Major.

Adrian Carton de Wiart was married and had children. He married Countess Friederike Maria Karoline Henriette Rosa Sabina Franziska Fugger von Babenhausen in 1912. They had four children together: two sons and two daughters

During World War I, Carton de Wiart's military career reached new heights. He fought in various major battles, including the Battle of the Somme and the Battle of Passchendaele. It was during these fierce conflicts that he exhibited extraordinary bravery and strength, earning him the nickname "Tough Old Boar" among his comrades. Despite being wounded many times and losing an eye and a hand in different engagements, he refused to leave the front lines and continued to serve with great courage.

After World War I, Carton de Wiart's military career continued to thrive. He held various high-ranking positions in the British Army and served in campaigns in the Middle East and Poland. He was appointed as the British Military Representative to the Supreme War Council in 1939, just before the outbreak of World War II.

In 1939, just before the outbreak of World War II, Carton de Wiart was appointed as Winston Churchill's personal representative to China, where he played a significant role in fostering relationships and coordinating with Chinese forces during the early stages of the conflict.

In 1940, he was appointed as the Head of the British Military Mission to Yugoslavia, where he worked to support and strengthen the Yugoslav resistance against Axis occupation. He was involved in aiding and advising the Partisans, the communist-led resistance forces under the leadership of Josip Broz Tito.

His military insight and diplomatic skills were important in building coalitions and supporting resistance movements.

Carton de Wiart's experiences during World War II were not limited to diplomatic and advisory roles. He actively participated in combat when the situation called for it. Despite his age and previous injuries, he was always ready to serve in the field.

Despite his diplomatic appointments, Adrian Carton de Wiart also fought in World War II. Although he was in his late 50s when the war began, his military experience and expertise made him a valuable asset. During World War II, Carton de Wiart held various important positions and served in different theaters of the war.

Carton de Wiart's military service during World War II was an extension of his lifelong commitment to duty and his unyielding responsibility to his countrymen. His presence and contributions during the war demonstrated his strong spirit and the valuable experience he brought to the table.

During World War II, Lieutenant General Adrian Carton de Wiart served in various theaters and participated in several significant battles and campaigns. Some of the notable battles and campaigns in which he was involved during World War II include:

The Battle of France (1940): Carton de Wiart served as Winston Churchill's representative to China during the early part of the war. However, after the fall of France, he was appointed to the British Military Mission in Yugoslavia.

The Balkans Campaign (1941): Carton de Wiart was in Yugoslavia during this period and played a role in supporting the Yugoslav Partisans against Axis forces.

East African Campaign (1941): Carton de Wiart led a military mission to Ethiopia and assisted in organizing resistance against Italian forces during the East African Campaign.

North African Campaign (1942): Carton de Wiart served in North Africa as the British liaison officer to the Free French forces under General Charles de Gaulle.

Italian Campaign (1943-1945): Carton de Wiart took

part in the Italian Campaign, serving as the head of the British Military Mission to the Yugoslav Partisans.

Second Battle of El Alamein (1942): Carton de Wiart was present during this crucial battle in North Africa, which marked a turning point in the Western Desert Campaign.

Battle of Monte Cassino (1944): Carton de Wiart's involvement in the Italian Campaign included the Battle of Monte Cassino, one of the most fiercely contested battles of the war.

Here s a scene from a war room in London during World War II. Winston Churchill, the British Prime Minister, sat at the head of the table, surrounded by military advisors and commanders. Adrian Carton de Wiart is standing waiting, his eye patch and missing hand a testament to his previous battlefield experiences. The room is tense, as they discuss the upcoming battle.

"Gentlemen, we stand on the precipice of a crucial moment in this war. Our next move will shape the course of history." Winston Churchill paused and looked at Carton de Wiart.

"Adrian, I value your counsel immensely. You've been part of innumerable battles, and your insight is invaluable.

"Thank you, Prime Minister. I'm honored to be here and ready to offer my thoughts."

"Excellent. We're faced with a challenging situation in the Italian theater. The Germans have entrenched themselves fiercely at Monte Cassino, and it seems impenetrable."

"Ah, Monte Cassino. A formidable fortress indeed, Prime Minister. To breach their defenses, we'll need to combine precision, deception, and raw power."

"I agree. It must be a multi-faceted attack, utilizing every resource at our disposal. General Alexander, what's your assessment?"

"Prime Minister, the enemy has heavily fortified the monastery on the hill. Our artillery bombardments haven't succeeded in dislodging them." General Alexander assessed the situation.

"We can't allow them to have a stronghold there. We must neutralize their position." Churchill said firmly.

"I suggest a feint in the south to divert their attention. While they focus there, we launch a full-scale attack from the north." Carton de Wiart said decisively.

"A feint, you say? That could deceive them, allowing us to gain the element of surprise. But will it be enough?" Churchill commented.

"If we hit them hard and fast from the north, utilizing the element of surprise, we stand a chance to catch them off-guard."

"I like the boldness of this plan. General Alexander, what are your thoughts?" Churchill commented

"The feint could work, Prime Minister. We could muster our forces for the northern assault while diverting their attention to the south." General Alexander agreed.

"Then let's move forward with this plan. Adrian, I'm putting you in charge of the northern assault. Your experience will be crucial in leading our forces." Churchill sounded satisfied.

"I won't disappoint you, Prime Minister. I'll lead our men with all the determination and skill I can muster.

"I know you won't, Adrian. Your tenacity is unmatched. Now, gentlemen, let's finalize the details of our plan. This battle will be a testament to the strength and resolve of the Allied forces. We shall not waver, and victory will be ours.

The room is filled with a renewed sense of purpose as they delve into the planning details, each knowing the weight of their responsibilities. The battle of Monte Cassino looms ahead, but with Churchill's strategic leadership and Carton de Wiart's battle-hardened experience, they are determined to overcome the challenges that lie ahead.

It's interesting to note that with experienced "career soldiers" like Carton de Wiart a combination of courage, experience, and strategy is adopted. You don't find the almost sacrificial passion of young soldiers who are prepared to throw their lives away but the strategic, practical approach works to save lives on a broad scale.

Throughout his military career in World War II, Carton de Wiart illustrated his dedication, bravery, and versatility as a military leader and diplomat. He played a substantial role in supporting various resistance movements and coordinating with Allied forces across different theaters of the war. Despite his age and previous injuries, he remained actively engaged in the confrontations and contributed his valuable experience to the Allied war effort.

By the end of his career, Carton de Wiart had been promoted to the rank of Lieutenant General and was awarded several prestigious honors, including the Victoria Cross, the Distinguished Service Order, and the Order of the British Empire.

In addition to his military accomplishments, Carton de Wiart was known for his colorful attitude, sense of humor, and adventurous spirit. He enjoyed big-game hunting and even survived a plane crash in a remote area of Turkey in 1940, which he, in his characteristic light-hearted manner, he described as a "pleasant" experience.

Adrian Carton de Wiart was a colorful character with a sense of humor. Here are a few entertaining facts about him

Despite surviving numerous injuries in his military career, including the loss of an eye and a hand, he once joked, "Frankly, I had enjoyed the war."

He was known for his adventurous spirit and love for hunting. At one point, he managed to capture a live crocodile during the Anglo-Egyptian War, which he intended to send to the London Zoo as a gift. However, the crocodile proved to be quite a handful and ended up escaping during the journey.

4. During his time as a prisoner of war in World War II,

he made several escape attempts. On one occasion, when asked why he kept trying to escape despite facing harsh punishments, he humorously replied, "It's rather exciting, really, but I'm getting too old for it."

Carton de Wiart was known for his unorthodox appearance, often described as rugged and eccentric. He had a distinctive eye patch and a thick beard, which added to his unique persona.

He was certainly larger than life in every way.

AFTER THE WAR

Adrian Carton de Wiart retired from the military in 1947 but remained active in public life and served in various governmental and diplomatic capacities. He passed away on June 5, 1963, at the age of 83, leaving behind a legacy of remarkable courage, resilience, and dedication to duty. His life and career remain an inspiration to many, a true testament to the indomitable spirit of a soldier who faced adversity with unwavering fortitude.

Pavlichenko's fame reached the status of legends and there were popular songs and poems written about her in both the Soviet Union and the United States.

Lyudmila Pavlichenko's life and achievements remain an inspiring testament to the courage and determination of women who played a significant role in World War II and history at large.

10

THE BATTLE OF STALINGRAD

LYUDMILA MIKHAILOVNA PAVLICHENKO A LEGENDARY SOVIET SNIPER

Lyudmila Mikhailovna Pavlichenko was born on 12 July 1916, in Belaya Tserkov, a town in the Kyiv Governorate of the Russian Empire which is now part of Ukraine. She grew up in a working family of Ukrainian and Russian heritage and developed an enthusiasm for shooting and marksmanship from a young age.

At the age of 14, Pavlichenko joined a local shooting club, where she sharpened her shooting skills and quickly became a skilled sharpshooter. She was married at 16 and had a son who was raised by her parents. She was divorced soon after his birth.

She studied history at Kyiv University before enlisting in the Red Army's 25th Rifle Division.

Her talent with a rifle soon caught the attention of military officials, and in 1937, she was accepted into the Soviet Union's Red Army as a sniper.

"During her sniper training, she impressed her instructors by consistently hitting her targets. When asked how she managed to be so accurate, she said, "There are no tricks to it. It's just practice.

Pavlichenko was the most successful female sniper in history, with over 300 confirmed kills. She received the nickname "Lady Death" for her deadly accuracy on the battlefield.

Later on in life, Pavlichenko would become a strong supporter of gender equality and women's rights. She used her fame to push for the creation of female sniper training schools in the Soviet Union.

DURING THE WAR

During World War II, Pavlichenko served as a sniper in the 25th Rifle Division of the Red Army. She fought in some of the most important battles of the Eastern Front, including the Siege of Odesa and the Battle of Sevastopol. Pavlichenko's skills as a sniper were unmatched, and she earned a reputation as one of the deadliest snipers of the war.

In 1942, Pavlichenko was sent to the United States and the United Kingdom as part of a Soviet delegation to get additional support for the war effort by persuading the Allies to open a second front. She spoke wherever she could get an audience to plead her cause. The American press refused to take her seriously, finding this hard-faced woman in a battle-stained uniform an affront to her sex. Nonetheless, Pavlichenko defended herself saying she was proud of her uniform which had often been bloodstained and was decorated with its medals of honor. She showed disdain for the American woman soldiers with their makeup, shorter skirts, and silk underwear

During her time in these countries, she became the first Soviet citizen to be received by a U.S. president, when she met with Franklin D. Roosevelt. She also addressed the British public and shared her experiences as a female soldier on the Eastern Front.

While in the United States, she was invited to a hunting trip in Oregon. She outperformed experienced hunters, leaving them astonished by her shooting skills.

On one occasion, when a group of American servicemen was skeptical about her being a sniper, she offered to illustrate her skills. She set up a target at 300 yards and easily hit four bullseyes in a row, quelling any doubts about her proficiency

The Battle of Stalingrad was a key and brutal military conflict during World War II, fought between Nazi Germany and the Soviet Union. It took place from 23 August 1942 to 2 February 1943, in the city of Stalingrad, which is situated in present-day Volgograd, Russia.

It was a highly important battle often thought of as one of the turning points of World War II. The Soviet victory in Stalingrad was a major setback for Nazi Germany and had crucial consequences for the rest of the war.

Stalingrad was of high strategic importance. Adolf Hitler sought to seize Stalingrad to control the city's industrial reserves and cut off the Soviet Union's crucial oil supplies from the region of the Caucasus.

The battle was one of the bloodiest and most violent in human history. It involved huge casualties on both sides, with estimates indicating that over two million people were killed, wounded, or captured.

Stalingrad was fiercely fought for, with much of the fighting taking place in the city's roads, factories, and buildings. Both sides engaged in house-to-house combat, resulting in high civilian fatalities and the near-total destruction of the city. This, as you can imagine, was a perfect situation for a sniper and Lyudmila Pavlichenko made the most of the opportunity.

The Soviet defenders, led by General Vasily Chuikov, exhibited remarkable resilience and courage in holding off the German forces. They endured brutal conditions and fought fiercely to protect the city.

As winter set in, the German Sixth Army, led by General Friedrich Paulus, became surrounded and trapped in the city by the encircling Soviet forces. Despite Hitler's orders to fight to the last man, Paulus eventually surrendered on 2 February 1943, marking an important defeat for the German military.

The Battle of Stalingrad became an important symbol of

Soviet resistance and the spirit of the Red Army. It played a crucial role in improving morale both in the Soviet Union and among the Allied forces.

The Soviet victory at Stalingrad marked the beginning of the Soviet Union's counteroffensive and eventually led to the pushback of German forces on the Eastern Front, ending in their defeat in 1945. The battle's effect on the war's outcome cannot be overstated, making it one of the most important events in World War II.

There would have been quite a bit of planning on how to make the battle of Stalingrad count against the German forces and as the key sniper Lyudmila Pavlichenko would have been central to this planning.

Imagine the scene at a makeshift command post in the heart of Stalingrad during the intense Battle of Stalingrad. Lyudmila Pavlichenko, the renowned Soviet sniper, was joined by her fellow officers and commanders, as they huddled together to discuss their next moves.

"Comrades, we find ourselves in the heart of this fierce battle. The enemy is brutal, and they have thrown everything at us. But we will not fail." Lyudmila Pavlichenko said with determination.

"You're right, Pavlichenko. Your prowess as a sniper has made a substantial impact on this battle. Your kills have struck fear into the hearts of the enemy," her commanding officer agreed.

"Thank you, Comrade. But this is a team effort. We all

play our part in defending Stalingrad and our Motherland."

"What's our next move, Pavlichenko? The Germans are still pressing hard from the western front." A junior officer asked eagerly.

"Our defense here is crucial. We've managed to hold them back so far, but we can't afford to be complacent. We need to continue disrupting their activities and targeting their key positions."

"Agreed. The enemy's snipers have been a thorn in our side. Pavlichenko, your expertise will be invaluable in neutralizing them, " the senior officer confirmed.

"I'll continue to prioritize taking out their snipers. But we must also be mindful of our safety. The Germans will be seeking revenge for their fallen comrades."

"What about our supplies, Comrade? We can't sustain this defense if we run low on ammunition and food." The junior officer sounded concerned.

"You're right. We need to maintain our supply lines at all costs. Let's designate a team to ensure our troops are well-equipped and well-fed." Lyudmila Pavlichenko agreed.

"Additionally, we should use our snipers to identify and disrupt enemy supply routes. Every disruption to their logistics weakens their offensive." The senior officer addressed the group but he looked at Lyudmila, as he spoke.

"Indeed. We can target their transport trucks and supply depots. The more disruption, the better."

"What about a counter-attack? Should we consider pushing back against their frontline?" The junior officer asked curiously.

"Not yet. We need to bide our time and conserve our strength. The Germans are relentless, but they are also overextended. Let's wait for the right moment to strike."

"Wise words, Pavlichenko. Patience and precision will be our allies," the senior officer agreed.

"Stalingrad will not fall. We will defend this city, street by street, building by building. The enemy may be strong, but we are stronger in spirit and determination. This is our land." Lyudmila Pavlichenko spoke prophetically.

The group nodded in agreement, steeling themselves for the challenges ahead. There was intense determination in their eyes that reflected the persistent resolve of the defenders of Stalingrad. With Pavlichenko's expertise and leadership, they stood ready to face whatever the Battle of Stalingrad threw their way.

Throughout her military service, Pavlichenko recorded an astonishing number of kills, with her confirmed kills tallying over 300, including 36 enemy snipers. No wonder her enemies were afraid of meeting up with "Lady Death."

At the age of 25, she married fellow sniper Alexei Kitsenko. They spent their honeymoon killing Germans. He was fatally wounded soon after and the battle came even more personal to the bereaved Pavlichenko. After returning to the Eastern Front, Pavlichenko continued to battle with distinction, but in June 1942, she was seriously wounded by mortar fire and was pulled from active combat duty. Due to her injuries, she was reassigned to a training position, where she continued to teach and inspire other snipers.

In 1943 she received the Gold Star of the Hero of the Soviet Union and the Order of Lenin

When asked about how she felt during combat, she reacted with her characteristic wit, saying, "I feel calm when I see the Germans. If they are there, then everything is fine. If I don't see them, then I begin to get nervous."

AFTER THE WAR

After the war, Lyudmila Pavlichenko completed her education and earned a degree in history from Kyiv University. She later pursued a career in academia, working as a historian and becoming involved in the Soviet Committee of War Veterans.

Lyudmila Pavlichenko passed away on 10 October 1974, at the age of 58 from a stroke. She had been suffering from PTSD and alcoholism. Her legacy as a heroic and skilled sniper, as well as a pioneer for women in the military, remains an inspiring and crucial part of World War II history. Her life and achievements continue to be commemorated in Russia and beyond, celebrating the bravery of one of the deadliest snipers in the history of warfare.

Pavlichenko's fame reached the status of legends and

there were popular songs and poems written about her in both the Soviet Union and the United States.

Lyudmila Pavlichenko's life and achievements remain an inspiring testament to the courage and determination of women who played a significant role in World War II and history at large.

WORKS CITED

- Kelly E, 22 Air Heroes and the Superhuman Stories that put them in the History Books. Updated 11 November 2022 https://allthatsinteresting.com/war-heroes
- Wikipedia Edited June 2023. https://en.wikipedia.org/wiki/John_Basilone
- Wikipedia Edited April 2023. https://en.m.wikipedia.org/wiki/Violette_Szabo
- Tillman B, Samurai of the Air, 4 December 2018. https://www.historynet.com/samurai-of-the-air/
- Mig Flug Best Fighter Pilots of All Time. Updated 2023. https://migflug.com/jetflights/ best-fighter-pilots-of-all-time/#:~:text= Erich%20Hartmann%20is%20the%20most, called%20%E2%80%9CThe%20black%20devil% E2%80%9D.
- Preskar P. The Formidable Simo Hayha - The Finnish Sniper Nicknamed White Death, 19 December 2022. https://short-history.com/simo-hayha-sniper-white -death-6d86663ee84c
- National WW2 Museum. Lady Death of the Red Army - Lyudmila Pavlichenko. 22 March 2021. https://www.nationalww2museum.org/war/articles /lady-death-red-army-lyudmila-pavlichenk.
- Linge MK. Soviet Girl Sniper had 309 Kills - and a best friend in the White House. 12 May 2018. https://nypost-com.cdn.ampproject.org/v/s/ nypost.com/2018/05/12/soviet-girl-sniper-had-309 -kills-and-a-best-friend-in-eleanor-roosevelt/amp/? amp_gsa=1&amp_js_v=a9&usqp= mq331AQIUAKwASCAAgM%3D#amp_tf= From%20%251%24s&aoh=16907270307026&

referrer=https%3A%2F%2Fwww.google.com&
ampshare=https%3A%2F%2Fnypost.com%2F2018
%2F05%2F12%2Fsoviet-girl-sniper-had-309-kills-
and-a-best-friend-in-eleanor-roosevelt%2F

- Reider E, Lady Death and the First Lady, 23 February
  2022,
  https://www.nps.gov/vama/blogs/lady-death-and-
  the-first-lady.htm#:~:text=Lyudmila%
  20Pavlichenko%20passed%20away%20in,while%
  20she%20was%20still%20alive.
- Wikipedia, Flying Ace, Updated 2023.
  https://en.m.wikipedia.org/wiki/Flying_ace#:~:text
  =Erich%20Hartmann%2C%20with%20352%
  20official,1%E2%81%842%20or%2026.83.
- Home of Heroes, World War II, Updated 2022.
  https://homeofheroes.com/heroes-stories/world
  -war-ii/
- Wikipedia, Women in World II, Updated 2023
  https://en.m.wikipedia.org/wiki/Women_in_
  World_War_II
- Pruitt S in History, Women in World War II took on
  these Dangerous Military Jobs, 1 March 2021.
  https://www.history.com/news/women-wwii-
  military-combat-front-lines
- Military.com, The most Legendary Snipers of all
  Time, 16 May 2019.
  https://www.military.com/off-duty/2019/05/16/5
  -most-legendary-snipers-all-time.html
- SAHO, Sir Winston Spencer Churchill, Updated 23
  August 2018
- https://www.sahistory.org.za/people/sir-winston-
  spencer-churchill
- BBC News Adrian Carton de Wiart - the unkillable
  soldier, 6 January 2015
- https://www.bbc.com/news/magazine-30685433

Don't Forget Your Free Bonus Downloads!

As our way of saying thank you, we've included in every purchase bonus gift downloads. If you've enjoyed reading this book, please consider leaving a review.

Or Scan Your Phone to open QR code

Afterword

Dear Reader,

We hope you enjoyed reading one of our favorite publications released so far - **The Veterans Memoir: True Combat Stories from World War II**. We hope it met and exceeded your expectations.

Want a free copy of our most recommended book on Amazon.com? For a limited time, we are offering a FREE gift to readers who leave a Customer Review on Amazon for the book you just enjoyed reading. This will help spread the word for others to discover this book.

Delivery is also instant to your inbox so you can receive your gift absolutely free.

To submit a review and get your free gift:

1. Go to the product detail page for the book on Amazon.com.
2. Click **Write a customer review** in the Customer Reviews section.
3. Click **Submit.**

*We would appreciate a lengthier review, but **any** review will qualify for our free gift!*

 Scan the QR code with your smartphone

Once you've submitted your Customer Review, email us at irvinepress@mail.com and we will send out the gift to you - pronto.

Best wishes,

*Check out the most recommended book on our Amazon.com's author page.

About Us

Modern Daily Press focuses on crafted material especially for kids through subjects that captivate young minds - think action, adventure, and everything that sparks their curiosity!

From tales of epic battles to thrilling military adventures, we're on a mission to provide books that have the power to shape young minds, and our commitment to producing high-quality content reflects our dedication to nurturing the love for reading and learning in boys. Our team of passionate writers, editors, and illustrators work tirelessly to create books that not only entertain but also inspire.

Click the +Follow button on our Author Page to stay updated on our latest releases So, join us as we embark on a journey of exploration and discovery!

Thank you,

Printed in Great Britain
by Amazon

60267066R00068